THE KREGEL PICTORIAL GUIDE TO

THE LIFE OF JESUS

Rob J. Bewley

Kregel Publications

I0809718

Published by Kregel Publications, a
division of Kregel, Inc., PO Box 2607,
Grand Rapids, MI 49501.

ISBN 978-0-8254-2494-6

Printed in Singapore

Picture Acknowledgements

Photographs
The Bridgeman Art Library: p. 29
Tim Dowley: pp. 8/9, 10 bottom right,
10/11, 13, 14, 15 top right, 19, 20/21, 30
Peter Wyart: pp. 5 (nos. 3, 4, 6), 6, 8,
12, 15 top left and bottom, 16, 21 inset,
22, 24/25, 24, 26

Illustrations
Shirley Bellwood: p. 17
Jeremy Gower: p. 5
Alan Parry: pp. 12/13
J. J. Tissot: pp. 18, 19, 22, 23, 27

Maps
Hardlines (except p. 31 top)

Also in the Kregel Pictorial Guide Series

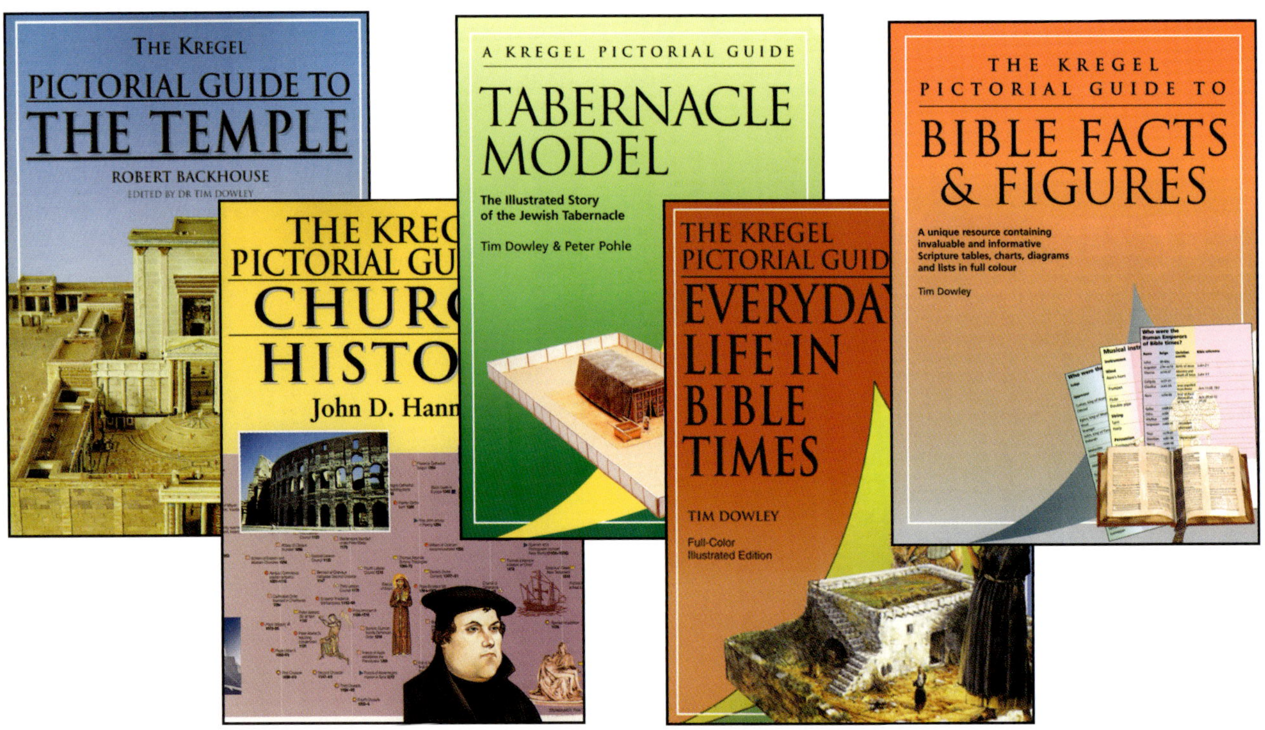

Contents

Introducing Jesus

Jesus Christ has to be the most influential person who has ever lived. The name Jesus comes from the Hebrew/Aramaic name Yeshua, the name given to Jesus when he was a week old. The word Christ comes from a Greek word meaning Messiah or Anointed One. So Christ is not his surname, but a way of proclaiming Jesus to be anointed and specially chosen.

Much about Jesus does not fit with the idea of someone who is specially chosen. He lived two thousand years ago in an obscure corner of the Roman Empire, spent most of his life in a very small community, held no political office, wrote nothing, and died while still in his thirties. Yet, in spite of that, he has been worshipped by billions of Christians over the centuries as the Son of God. Those of other faiths also normally hold him in high regard; for instance, Muslims recognize him as a great prophet. Even those of no faith at all tend to accept much of his teaching as valuable.

Although there have been, from time to time, scholars who have denied even that Jesus existed, nearly all historians today, whether Christian or not, accept that there is overwhelming evidence, both in the Bible and elsewhere, that he did exist. Indeed we know much more about Jesus than about most other characters from that time.

What did Romans say?

Roman writers did not tend to be very interested in what was going on at the far eastern edge of the Empire, and so we should not be too surprised that they do not provide us with much information about Jesus. The Roman historian Tacitus refers to Christians in his description of the fire of Rome in A.D. 64, and says that they got their name from Christ, the one who was executed by Pilate. Sadly the portion of Tacitus' Annals that covers the time of the ministry of Jesus has not survived. Lucian of Samosata also refers later to Christians worshipping 'that great man who was crucified in Palestine'. Pliny the Younger writes of Christians meeting to sing to Christ as a god, and Suetonius blames the riots in Rome in A.D. 49 on people following the teachings of Christ. (He refers to Chrestus but this may be a variant spelling of Christus.)

So Roman writers confirm that Jesus lived, died under Pontius Pilate and was then worshipped by many, but they do not tell us much about Jesus' life.

Josephus describes Jesus

"At this time there was a wise man called Jesus, and his conduct was good, and he was known to be virtuous. Many people among the Jews and the other nations became his disciples. Pilate condemned him to be crucified and to die. But those who had become his disciples did not abandon his discipleship. They reported that he had appeared to them three days after his crucifixion and that he was alive. Accordingly, he was perhaps the Messiah, concerning whom the prophets have reported wonders. And the tribe of Christians, so named after him, has not disappeared to this day."

(Josephus: *Antiquities* 18:63-64)

A very early fragment of John's Gospel.

The Roman Empire

Tacitus explains about "Christians"

"They got their name from Christ, who was executed by sentence of the procurator Pontius Pilate in the reign of Tiberias. The pernicious superstition, suppressed for the moment, broke out again, not only throughout Judea, the birthplace of the plague, but also in the city of Rome." (Tacitus: *Annals* 15:44)

What did Jews say?

There are a couple of passages in the Jewish writings called the Talmud that probably refer to Jesus. They talk of him practicing magic and leading Israel astray. However, our most significant Jewish source is the historian Josephus, who wrote, among other things, a major work called Jewish Antiquities. This includes a couple of more extensive references to Jesus. Some scholars believe that later Christian copyists added bits to his original texts, but, even if these bits are removed, Josephus still describes Jesus as a wise man, who did surprising deeds, taught people, was condemned to the cross by Pilate, and who continues to be worshipped. At one point, he refers to Jesus as the so-called Messiah—the sort of thing you would expect from someone who was not a Christian.

So Jewish writers add a bit more detail about Jesus' life, but for more information we must turn to Christian writers.

What did early Christians say?

We have four accounts of Jesus' life in the Bible—those of Matthew, Mark, Luke, and John. Given the degree of overlap between them, scholars have, over the centuries, come up with many different theories to explain the relationship between their accounts. Perhaps the most likely explanation is that Mark wrote the first and shortest account, and that Matthew and Luke had access to Mark's Gospel, but felt that they knew additional things about Jesus which were not included. For example, they each include information about Jesus' birth, which was presumably not important for Mark, and also add more of Jesus' teaching. John tells the story in a very different way, with much longer speeches and reflections.

We are very fortunate to have four accounts to broaden our understanding. It is rather like hearing four different people telling us about a party or a football match—we learn much more than if only one person has told us. These are not the only versions of Jesus' life that were written, but it is generally accepted that the others are either corrupted forms of the four we already have, or later products of over-developed imaginations! We can be grateful to the early church for the work done in establishing the reliability of the four Gospels in the Bible.

Is this the face of Jesus?

Jesus has been portrayed in many different ways across the centuries.

Jesus' Early Years

Cutaway illustration of the interior of a peasant's house in the time of Jesus.

We know very little about Jesus' early years. Two of the four Gospel writers (evangelists) in the Bible (Mark and John) do not mention anything about Jesus' life before he is an adult, and we have no record of Jesus' talking about his childhood. Matthew's account leaps straight from infancy to adulthood, and Luke only includes one story about Jesus as an adolescent. At the time it was normal not to give an account of childhood in the story of a great man, for it was considered less important than his adult exploits. Nevertheless, we must conclude that, for the most part, Jesus' upbringing was fairly normal for a Jewish boy of that period.

Where there is a hole, people tend to fill it. Later writers tried to fill in fanciful stories about Jesus' childhood, but these stories are clearly not reliable. Anyone who has ever been to a Nativity play, looked at Christmas cards, or sung Christmas carols has been exposed to so many layers of tradition that have been added to the original stories that it is easy to lose sight of the historical core at the center of it all.

Who were Jesus' parents?

Joseph was a carpenter, stonemason, or some form of builder (the Greek word *teknōn* does not imply that he necessarily worked with wood). Although his ancestry could be traced right back to King David, we know that he was not wealthy, for when, in keeping with Jewish law, Mary and he presented a sacrifice in thanks for the gift of their son, they presented the type designed for the poor (Luke 2:24).

But Joseph was not Jesus' biological father. He was already engaged to the young girl Mary when she became pregnant. He was tempted to call it off, but learned in a dream what Mary had been told before she became pregnant, namely that the father was none other than God's Holy Spirit.

A simple dwelling in Nazareth, not unlike the houses Jesus would have known.

When was Jesus born?

Jesus was probably born about 5 or 4 B.C. This may seem a little strange, given that the dating system is supposed to revolve around his birth, but the calendar as we know it was not put together until the sixth century under Pope John I. The consensus is that the man doing it (a monk called Dionysius) simply miscalculated. We come to this conclusion because of various factors, including what we know from elsewhere about the date of Herod the Great's death, the possible date of a census, Jesus' approximate age when he began his ministry, as well as historical dating (Luke 3), and the possibility of certain natural phenomena accounting for the Magi's journey.

Where was Jesus born?

Because of a government census, Joseph and Mary had to travel to Bethlehem, near Jerusalem, from their home in Nazareth. It was while they were there that Jesus was born. Jesus' first resting place was a manger, "because there was no place for them in the *kataluma* [guest room, house or inn]" (Luke 2:7). Bethlehem would have been overfull with visitors, but it is unlikely that there would have been an inn as such. The most plausible explanation is that the family had to cram into the tiny home of relatives, but, because the guest room was already full, they had to use the part of the house in which the animals slept. This was still a very humble, uncomfortable beginning.

Prophecy	Fulfillment
Look, the virgin is with child and shall bear a son, and shall name him Immanuel. (Is. 7:14)	Look, the virgin shall conceive and bear a son, and they shall name him Emmanuel. (Mt.1:23)
But you, O Bethlehem of Ephrathah, who are one of the little clans of Judah, from you shall come forth for me one who is to rule in Israel. (Mic. 5:2)	And you, Bethlehem, in the land of Judah, are by no means least among the rulers of Judah; for from you shall come a ruler who is to shepherd my people Israel. (Mt. 2:6)
When Israel was a child, I loved him, and out of Egypt I called my son. (Hos. 11:1)	This was to fulfil what had been spoken by the Lord through the prophet, "Out of Egypt I have called my son." (Mt. 2:15)
A voice is heard in Ramah, lamentation and bitter weeping. Rachel is weeping for her children; she refuses to be comforted for her children, because they are no more. (Jer. 31:15)	Then was fulfilled what had been spoken through the prophet Jeremiah: "A voice was heard in Ramah, wailing and loud lamentation, Rachel weeping for her children; she refused to be consoled, because they are no more." (Mt. 2:17-18)

Reactions to the birth

Luke tells us that some shepherds (who would normally be considered as unclean, marginalized peasants) responded to a visit by angels and were the first to visit the newborn infant. He also tells us about two righteous and devout people, Simeon and Anna. When they saw the week-old Jesus at the Temple in Jerusalem, they knew that he was someone very special.

Matthew tells of the visit of some Magi. We do not know how many of them there were, and they were not kings but star-watchers, who came from a long way away, guided by unusual activity in the night sky. They searched long and hard for Jesus, brought him gifts, and also recognized Jesus as someone very special.

Right from the start of Jesus' life, there were people who recognized him as someone special, while others rejected him.

Growing up

Jesus grew up in the village of Nazareth, presumably learning Joseph's trade. When he was twelve, his parents lost him on the way back from their annual trip up to Jerusalem. They eventually found him in the Temple, sitting with religious teachers and asking them questions. He seemed to have some sort of awareness of his relationship to God the Father, but was still growing, inquiring, and learning like any boy.

The Song of Simeon

Master, now you are dismissing
your servant in peace,
according to your word;
for my eyes have seen your
salvation,
which you have prepared in the
presence of all peoples,
a light for revelation to the
Gentiles
and for glory to your people
Israel.
(Luke 2:29-32)

Jesus' Ministry in Galilee

Baptism and temptation

We know nothing more of Jesus' life until he burst onto the scene in his early thirties. A prophet called John was announcing the coming of the day of the Lord, calling people to turn away from their sins and baptizing them in the River Jordan. Although Jesus did not need to turn away from sin, he too underwent baptism, as a sign of solidarity with the people. The Gospels record that this was a powerful spiritual experience for him, as the Holy Spirit descended on him to equip him for his ministry, and a heavenly voice declared him to be "my beloved son" (Mark 1:11 and parallels).

Left: Mosaic of a vessel on the Sea of Galilee, from Capernaum.

Jesus' ministry began with forty days in the wilderness, a period which acts as a reminder of the forty years that Moses and the people of Israel wandered through the wilderness, after they escaped from Egypt and before they settled in the Promised Land. During this period we read that Jesus fasted and was tempted/tested by the devil to misuse his power and authority. But he resisted and returned from the desert, ready to begin his ministry. However one interprets this period of testing, it is a sign of spiritual opposition occurring early on, opposition that would continue throughout Jesus' public life.

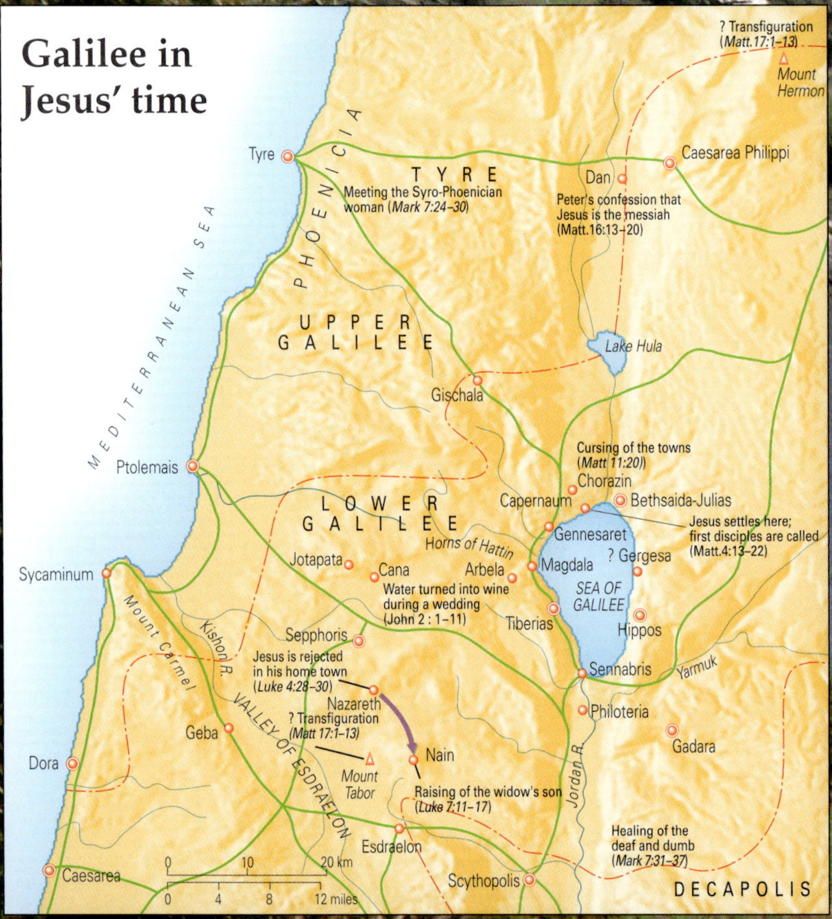

An itinerant and rural ministry

The accounts of this public life do not allow us to be completely certain about its length, but it seems most likely that Jesus was active in his ministry for a maximum of three years. Most of this time was spent in the region of Galilee, the name given to the region to the west of the Sea of Galilee, which was administered separately from Judea further south. The region was predominantly Jewish, but there was a significant non-Jewish (Gentile) population in the cities of Sepphoris and Tiberias. Jesus is not recorded as having spent any time in these cities, and rarely went to his home town of Nazareth. On the only occasion we hear of him visiting Nazareth, the reception was somewhat hostile (Mark 6:1-6). Instead, he based himself in the fishing village of Capernaum. From there he travelled primarily around the countryside and small communities of Galilee, although he also went beyond its borders on several occasions.

He did not travel alone. Like many religious leaders of his day, Jesus gathered around him a collection of disciples. But the people he chose were not learned; they were simple people from a variety of backgrounds, who were so impressed by his presence that they left everything and followed him. He chose twelve to be particularly close to him, a number which is significant because it recalls the number of the tribes of Israel. It is as if Jesus was reconstituting Israel around himself.

Overall: **A replica sailing vessel of Jesus' time approaches the site of biblical Capernaum on the Sea of Galilee.**

Teaching and opposition

We will examine the different aspects of Jesus' ministry in later chapters, but it focused on three primary things. He taught about the Kingdom of God, he healed people from a wide range of sicknesses, and he released people who were oppressed by evil spirits. As his reputation grew, everywhere that Jesus went people flocked to him for healing, exorcism, or teaching. On one occasion the number gathered is counted at five thousand men, as well as women and children.

But Jesus was not popular with everyone. Although he was faithful to the teachings of the Jewish Bible, his interpretations were sometimes at odds with those of the religious leaders of the day. Unlike the scribes, he appeared to speak with authority (Matthew 7:29), even though he had no official or recognized authority. The scribes and Pharisees, who were the learned devout teachers of the Law, liked neither his popularity nor the way in which he broke many of their laws, and very soon they started to think of ways in which they could get rid of him.

Jesus, Jerusalem, and the Temple

Jerusalem

Then, as now, Jerusalem was the political, religious, and social center of the Jewish world. At Jerusalem's center stood the Temple, which dominated the city both physically and economically. There had been a Temple in Jerusalem on and off since the tenth century B.C. It was considered to be the very dwelling-place of God on earth. Two previous Temples had been destroyed, but, in Jesus' time, there stood the magnificent and colossal structure, which Herod the Great had built largely before Jesus' birth, but on which extensive work continued. With all its courts and buildings, it measured nearly 500m x 300m. Professor Graham Stanton estimates that nearly half the population of the city depended on the Temple for their livelihood.

Three times a year the population swelled—perhaps as much as four-fold—as pilgrims came for the major Jewish feasts, and Roman soldiers were drafted in to quell any potential uprising.

Jesus spent very little time in Jerusalem. John records just a couple of visits, while the other Gospel writers make no mention of Jesus' going to Jerusalem before the final week of his life. But his time in Jerusalem was very important. Jesus was aware that he was going to face strong opposition there, and the Gospel writers devote a large proportion of their accounts of his life to the few days that he was there.

Jesus' entry into the city

Jesus' arrival in Jerusalem seemed to be calculated to attract as much attention as possible. He didn't simply walk into the city, but arranged to enter on a donkey. This detail might seem insignificant to us, but any devout Jew would have known that Zechariah 9:9 refers to Israel's King arriving in the city on a donkey. This was a highly symbolic act, and the crowd became very excited.

The Temple incident

The most significant action of the first part of the week was when Jesus went into the Temple, overturned the tables of money-changers, and drove out people who were selling things there. Scholars

This view of an authentic model of Jerusalem in the time of Jesus shows how Herod's Temple physically dominated the entire city.

View of Herod's Temple from the Jerusalem model.

have debated just what Jesus was trying to do. Some have suggested that he was trying to instigate an uprising, but this is not consistent with his teaching elsewhere, and it seems likely that the incident took place only in one corner of the enormous courtyard—otherwise it would have attracted the attention of the Roman guard.

The most commonly expressed explanation (supported by the subtitle of the section in many editions of the Bible) is that Jesus was enacting a kind of cleansing of the Temple. According to this thinking, Jesus was protesting against the activity of the money-changers, and wanted to restore pure worship at the Temple.

However, this interpretation is not without problems. The money-changers and sellers of ritually pure animals were an integral part of the activity of the Temple, for they were required to ensure that the Temple tax and the animals offered for sacrifice were clean and fit for the purpose. It therefore seems more likely that Jesus was acting out a parable against the very existence of the Temple. Later on, alone with his disciples, Jesus explicitly predicted the physical destruction of the Temple, destruction which would take place less than forty years later (Mark 13:1-4 and parallels).

Increasing opposition

Whatever was meant, the tension was raised between Jesus and the religious authorities. Over the following days, Jesus continued to teach in the Temple compound (Luke 21:37-38), but he told parables and made pronouncements which seemed to be increasingly offensive towards the authorities. In turn, they tried to catch him out by asking him questions which were designed to trick him into incriminating himself. But they did not succeed, and were afraid to arrest him openly, because he seemed to have the support of the crowd (Matthew 26:3-5 and Mark 14:1-2).

In the end, the solution to the authorities' problem came from the inside, when one of Jesus' inner ring of twelve disciples decided to betray him in return for a handsome reward. The scene was set for the most remarkable few days in the history of the world. . . .

Percentage of each Gospel devoted to Jesus' last week

Book	Total verses	Last week	Last week
Matthew	1069	389	36%
Mark	661	253	38%
Luke	1149	286	25%
John	879	332	38%

Jesus' Last Days

A special meal

Jesus assembled his twelve closest disciples to celebrate the Passover. There was nothing unusual about this. Except under exceptional circumstances, all adult Jews were expected to come to Jerusalem each year to celebrate Passover, and, in doing so, to recall the way in which God had saved his people from slavery in Egypt.

But Jesus seemed to take some of the key elements of the meal and give them new meaning. For the host to speak blessings over the food and wine would be normal, but Jesus went one stage further: he suggested that the bread and wine were his body and blood, and that, after his imminent death, his followers should use these elements of the meal to remember not the escape from Egypt, but his broken body and his spilled blood (Mark 14:22-25 and parallels).

There is a degree of doubt about whether the meal was a Passover, for, in John's account, the timing is slightly different. In one sense it does not matter. What is important is the new symbolic importance which Jesus gave to the meal. John's account of this last evening together includes a description of Jesus' choosing to undertake the most menial task of washing the feet of his disciples. In doing so, he offered a vividly counter-cultural instruction regarding the nature of leadership (John 13:14-15).

Anguish and arrest

Knowing that he was about to be betrayed by Judas, Jesus then went to a garden or olive grove called Gethsemane, just outside the city. In this garden we see Jesus struggling in a way in which we have not seen him before. He went off on his own to pray, but was disappointed when he returned to find Peter, James, and John sleeping. Jesus seemed to be very alone and agitated. The nature of his prayer reveals much about his anguish. All through his ministry, it was clear that he knew what his end was going to be, and yet he prayed fervently to his Father not to have to face what was to come. This is a

Jesus suggested that the bread and wine were his body and blood, and that, after his death, his followers should use them to remember his broken body and spilled blood.

The Church of the Holy Sepulchre, Jerusalem, traditionally regarded as the site of Jesus' crucifixion and burial.

picture of a real human being, feeling isolated from his friends, and fearful of the future. Yet there is an important conclusion to his yearning—that what matters most is not his personal wish but the Father's will (Mark 14:36 and parallels).

It was while Jesus was in the Garden of Gethsemane that his former disciple Judas arrived with an armed gang from the Temple authorities. After Jesus' arrest, there followed a series of trials. (Or at least "hearings"—many doubt whether these exchanges would have stood up to scrutiny as legal trials.)

The Sanhedrin (the religious council) found him guilty of blasphemy, and took him to the occupying Roman powers in the person of the governor, Pilate. It would appear that Pilate was not very interested in what he perceived to be a Jewish dispute, but he agreed to condemn Jesus on the charge of claiming to be King of the Jews, in order to keep the religious authorities happy. Such a claim could be construed to be both religious and political.

Jesus institutes Communion

While they were eating, Jesus took a loaf of bread, and after blessing it he broke it, gave it to the disciples, and said, "Take, eat; this is my body." Then he took a cup, and after giving thanks, he gave it to them, saying, "Drink from it, all of you; for this is my blood of the covenant, which is poured out for many for the forgiveness of sins".
(Mt. 26:26-28)

The end?

The death Jesus suffered was the worst kind known to the Roman authorities, normally reserved for particularly heinous crimes committed by non-Roman citizens. In crucifixion, the victim would be flogged and then attached to an upright cross of wood by nails through his wrists and feet. It was a slow, agonizing process; death came about through asphyxiation, as the victim suffered more and more pain from raising his body to get air into his lungs. The agony was made worse by the humiliation of being naked and open to abuse from passers-by. For a Jew it was even worse, for all Jews were aware that, according to Deuteronomy 21:23, anyone hung on a tree was under God's curse.

Depending on the individual crucified, it took anything from a few hours to several days for death to come. Jesus took just six hours to die, after which he was buried in the tomb of a supporter, rather than being placed in a common grave or left to be pecked at by birds, as was frequently the case. For the final three hours of suffering on the cross, there was darkness, and, as he died, the curtain in the Temple was torn in two (Matthew 27:51 and Mark 15:38). But, for an explanation of this, along with an understanding of how Jesus' death could be portrayed not only as tragedy, but also as triumph, we need to continue, for the story does not end with Jesus' death. . . .

Jesus Rises from the Dead

Back from the dead

In spite of the amazing things that Jesus did when he was alive, the most extraordinary, and arguably the most important, part of his story does not come until after his death. Jesus died on a Friday, the day before the Sabbath. After the Sabbath rest day, first thing on Sunday morning, two of Jesus' women supporters went to the tomb and were greeted by an extraordinary sight. The stone, which sealed the entrance to the tomb, had been rolled back and the tomb was empty. They saw some kind of figure, variously described as an angel or a man in a dazzling white garment, who informed them that Jesus had risen from the dead (Mark 16:1-8 and parallels).

The Gospel writers then record a variety of appearances by Jesus over a period of several weeks. He appeared to disciples as they cowered fearful in a locked room; he appeared to them when they were fishing; he appeared to a pair of dejected disciples who were walking from Jerusalem to a nearby village called Emmaus, and explained to them how all the things which had happened to him were in keeping with the promises of Scripture. He even appeared on one occasion to a gathering of five hundred people (1 Corinthians 15:6). The descriptions that we have of Jesus at this time suggest that his body was very real, yet also unique. He still had the wounds from his violent death, and he ate food, yet he was not always recognizable and seemed to be able to pass through locked doors.

You cannot be serious!

Did Jesus really rise from the dead? It is the single most important foundation of the Christian faith, and so it is not surprising that, over the centuries, there have been those who have been determined to deny that it really happened. But all alternative explanations fall down.

1. Some claim that Jesus had not actually died, but merely fainted and then recovered. But this explanation takes into account neither the violence done to Jesus' dead body (John 19:34) nor the problem of a man who had been unconscious for two days suddenly moving the enormous stone that sealed the entrance.

2. Others like to think that perhaps Jesus' disciples stole his corpse. However, such a feat would require overpowering or bribing trained Roman soldiers, and would surely be done in a rush that would not allow time to remove the grave clothes and fold them neatly. And would the disciples really have gone on to suffer all sorts of hardships and humiliations for proclaiming the resurrection, if they knew it was a fake?

3. A third suggestion made by some is that the disciples were hallucinating when they saw Jesus. But he appeared in a variety of ways to a large number of people—hardly the stuff of hallucinations. Even if they were hallucinations, it would have been the easiest thing in the world for the authorities to produce the body, in order to nip

Paul on the resurrection

For I handed on to you as of first importance what I in turn had received: that Christ died for our sins in accordance with the scriptures, and that he was buried, and that he was raised on the third day in accordance with the scriptures, and that he appeared to Cephas, then to the twelve. Then he appeared to more than five hundred brothers and sisters at one time, most of whom are still alive, though some have died.
(1 Cor. 15:3-6)

Pilgrims around the Garden Tomb, Jerusalem, remember Jesus' resurrection.

The Chapel of the Ascension, Mount of Olives, Jerusalem.

this troublesome new movement in the bud.

The stories about Jesus' resurrection have an air of authenticity about them, right down to the fact that, if you were trying to make something up, you would have made up something easier to defend. For example, women's testimony counted for nothing at that time in that culture, so why make the first eyewitnesses women if that is not what happened? The reason why people try so hard to disprove the resurrection is that its truth has enormous implications.

The characteristic domes of the Church of the Holy Sepulchre, Jerusalem.

What does it mean?

What are Jesus' death and resurrection all about? Theologians have debated this for centuries and come up with a variety of answers, most of which probably have a degree of truth about them. The most important significance was that Jesus, as a sinless human being, was paying the penalty for the wrong living of the rest of humankind, and thereby allowing God to welcome sinful people back into relationship with him. But he seems to have been doing more than that. His death was a kind of ransom (Matthew 20:28 and Mark 10:45) paid to buy freedom from sin, a revelation of God's love and a supreme example of sacrificial love. By rising from the dead, he also defeated death itself.

This tomb of the Herod family, Jerusalem, has a rolling-stone door similar to the tomb where Jesus was buried.

Final departure

The period of appearances came to an end after forty days. At that point Jesus instructed his disciples to make disciples of people all over the world, to baptize them and to teach them, secure in the knowledge that he would be with them by his Spirit. Luke's account says that Jesus told them first to wait, in order to receive the equipping of the Holy Spirit. So not only does Jesus' story continue past his death, but it also continues past his ascension. But before we consider that, let us go back and look at some aspects of Jesus' ministry in more detail.

Jesus' Identity

Who did Jesus think he was? Who did those around him think he was? Who was Jesus of Nazareth? To answer these questions, let us look at four titles that have been applied to him.

A wandering rabbi

In many respects Jesus was very much like the rabbis of his period, who roamed around, accompanied by disciples, dispensing advice and debating interpretations of the Law. But they tended to come from one of the recognized rabbinic schools, and to be sought out by disciples who would attach themselves to them. By contrast, in spite of Jesus' ability to speak with authority (Mark 1:22 and parallels), he appears to have had no such formal training, and was the one who took the initiative to gather his inner circle of twelve disciples around him.

Relief of Jesus praying before his arrest in the Garden of Gethsemane.

Messiah/Christ

By the time that the apostle Paul was writing, twenty years after Jesus' life, he was using the term Christos (which is simply the Greek word for Messiah) as a title for Jesus, as if it were his surname. But at the time of Jesus, Messiah would have had very different connotations. Jewish hopes and expectations regarding the arrival of a Messiah were complex and varied, but there was a significant stream of thought that hoped for the arrival of a great leader from the line of King David, who would come and deliver military victory over the occupying Roman powers and herald a new age of freedom and prosperity for Israel.

Jesus fulfils some, but not all, of these expectations. He came from David's line, he restored many to wholeness, he chose twelve disciples in a clear allusion to the twelve tribes of Israel, and he entered Jerusalem riding on a donkey in fulfilment of Zechariah 9:9. Yet, he had no intention of bringing about a military uprising, and, when one of his disciples acknowledged him as Messiah, he told him to hush it up (Mark 8:30 and parallels).

Church on Mount Tabor commemorating the transfiguration of Jesus.

Some scholars claim that Jesus had no Messianic pretensions at all, and that all references to his being Messiah are later inventions of the early church. But it would make no sense for the church to give him that title, if he hadn't made some reference to it himself; for, by not bringing about military victory and by dying an ignominious death, he had ultimately failed to meet the popular expectation of a Messiah.

So why did Jesus seem so reluctant to make the claim to be Messiah? This could be for a number of reasons:

1. There would be great political danger in making such a claim openly, for the occupying powers would be very sensitive to someone making claims to be a savior of the nation. (Although there is a degree of doubt regarding the exact wording of Jesus' statements at his trials, it is surely no coincidence that it is when Jesus is under arrest and knows that he is about to die that he is most open about his identity.)

2. Because Jesus' idea of a suffering Messiah was so different from popular conceptions, it would have led to misunderstanding.

3. There was a tradition that one could not claim to be Messiah until one had accomplished the Messiah's task. In Jesus' case, this was not until after he had died.

Son of God

At the time, the term son of God was sometimes used to refer to particularly special people or heavenly beings. Paul and other later New Testament writers spoke of the Son of God to refer to Jesus in a special relationship to God. Jesus never used the term himself, but the Gospels clearly record many references to Jesus' unique sonship.

Most significantly, on two occasions a voice from heaven described him to be "my beloved son". The first was at the beginning of his ministry, at his baptism (Mark 1:11 and parallels), and the second was at the extraordinary event known as the Transfiguration (Mark 9:7 and parallels). At this event, the disciples who were with Jesus saw his clothes become dazzling white, as he appeared to be joined by Moses and Elijah and then enveloped by a cloud. Jesus was also happy to talk about God as "my Father" (e.g. Matthew 11:27), and even referred to him by the familiar term, abba, whose closest translation is dad or daddy.

Artist's impression of a rabbi with the Torah scroll in an ancient synagogue.

Daniel's vision

I saw one like a human being [a son of man] coming with the clouds of heaven. And he came to the Ancient One and was presented before him. To him was given dominion and glory and kingship, that all peoples, nations, and languages should serve him. His dominion is an everlasting dominion that shall not pass away, and his kingship is one that shall never be destroyed.
(Daniel 7:13-14)

Son of Man

This was Jesus' favored way of talking about himself. Some scholars, such as Geza Vermes, see it as just another way of saying "I" or "a man like me". While there may be some truth in this in some instances, there must be more, given the heavenly associations of the term in Daniel 7 and some of the inter-testamental writings. Whatever its origins, it certainly helped Jesus to identify himself with humankind.

Jesus' Purpose

Artist's impression of Jesus reading from the Jewish scriptures at the synagogue.

The Gospel writers rarely take us into Jesus' mind to provide insights into his motivation, but we can infer a fair amount about Jesus' purposes from what he said and did. Some suggest that his sense of purpose developed over the time of his ministry. There may be some truth in this, but there is also good evidence for Jesus having a clear sense of purpose from the beginning.

We can perhaps do no better than go to the start of his ministry and examine what many have called "Jesus' manifesto" (Luke 4:16-21). The scene was the synagogue in Nazareth, Jesus' home town. As a normal part of worship, Jesus read a passage from the book of the prophet Isaiah. But he then proceeded to claim that certain things prophesied had come into being on that day. So what were these things?

Bringing good news to the poor

The first thing that Jesus spoke of was bringing good news to the poor. Jesus came to bring tangible relief to those who were economically disadvantaged, not only by providing food miraculously, but also by healing some whose infirmity meant that they were forced to beg for a living. He also came to offer future hope beyond the difficulties of this life.

Jesus came to bring hope to all those who were excluded from society; the materially poor were a major part, but not the only part, of this grouping. For example, in the story he told, Jesus offered acceptance and inclusion for the repentant tax collector in the Temple (Luke 18:9-14), while the lost and rejected Zacchaeus was welcomed back into society (Luke 19:1-10).

The other items in this manifesto are, in a sense, subcategories of the first, and each would seem to have both a literal and metaphorical meaning. Jesus proclaimed that he was going to offer release to those who were held captive by sin, and freedom for those who were oppressed by spirits and by unfair structures in society.

Jesus also proclaimed the recovery of sight to the blind. This clearly had a literal meaning, as Jesus healed blind people on many occasions (e.g., Mark 8:22-26; Mark 10:46-52 and parallels; John 9:1-7), but he also accused the teachers of the Law of

The Lord's Prayer

Our Father in heaven,
hallowed be your name.
Your kingdom come.
Your will be done,
on earth as it is in heaven.
Give us this day our daily bread.
And forgive us our debts,
as we also have forgiven our debtors.
And do not bring us to the time of trial,
but rescue us from the evil one.
(Matthew 6:9-13)

You have heard	I say to you
You shall not murder	If you are angry with a brother or sister you will be liable to judgement
You shall not commit adultery	Everyone who looks at a woman with lust has already committed adultery with her in his heart
Whoever divorces his wife, let him give her a certificate of divorce	Anyone who divorces his wife . . . causes her to commit adultery
You shall not swear falsely . . .	Do not swear at all
An eye for an eye and a tooth for a tooth . . .	Do not resist an evildoer
You shall love your neighbor	Love your enemies

Artist's impression of Jesus leading his disciples through the Galilean countryside.

being "blind guides", and wanted to open people's spiritual eyes in order that they might see the world differently.

Proclaiming the year of the Lord's favor

This phrase was linked to the concept of the year of Jubilee, during which debts would be written off. Jesus seemed to be going further than this through his talk of the Kingdom of God—God's rule in heaven coming into being on earth. For Jesus, this Kingdom was not the widely sought-after political one, in which Israel would be made free from occupation, but a Kingdom in which God ruled over creation and saved the afflicted. Jesus heralded this event as being in the future, and urged all to pray for it to come—"your kingdom come". Yet he also embodied many aspects of this Kingdom in terms of his control over demons, diseases, and natural forces. In Jesus' life (and in the subsequent activity of the Spirit), the Kingdom of God was revealed in part, but its full consummation must wait until the end of time.

Jesus' mission statement

The Spirit of the Lord is upon me, because he has anointed me to bring good news to the poor. He has sent me to proclaim release to the captives and recovery of sight to the blind, to let the oppressed go free, to proclaim the year of the Lord's favor.
(Luke 4:18-19)

A barren valley in the Judean hills.

Renewing Israel

Jesus was a faithful Jew, and insisted that he came not to abolish the Law but to fulfil it (Matthew 5:17). Nevertheless, he also carried out some radical reinterpretation of the Law (note the "you have heard it said . . . but I say to you" sayings of Matthew 5). In selecting twelve special disciples (twelve being the number of the tribes of Israel), in offering forgiveness outside of the Temple system, and in reinterpreting the Passover symbolism in relation to himself, it would appear that Jesus wanted to reshape what it meant to be Israel.

Dying for others

It is important not to reduce the purpose of Jesus' life simply to his death, but we cannot escape the fact that Jesus was aware that he was going to suffer death in Jerusalem at the hands of the authorities (Mark 8:31 and parallels; Mark 9:31 and parallels; Mark 10:33-34 and parallels), but he still pressed on to the city. He had a purpose to fulfil to "give his life as a ransom for many" (Matthew 20:28 and Mark 10:45). As a sinless human being, he chose to die to pay the penalty for the wrong living of the rest of humankind.

Jesus the Teacher

For many who are not followers of Jesus, he was primarily a great teacher, who dispensed universally applicable moral exhortation. But this is a pale reflection of Jesus for four reasons:

1. If he had taught as he did, but was not who he said he was, then he would have been deluded and dangerous.
2. If he had taught the things he did without facilitating the help of the Holy Spirit to enable the believer to obey, his counsel would have been too idealistic and remote.
3. His teaching covered topics that went beyond the merely ethical.
4. Jesus' ministry consisted of more than just teaching—he also healed, exorcized, and worked some extraordinary miracles.

Nevertheless, his teaching was important and radical, and remains so to this day.

Content of Jesus' teaching

It is impossible to do justice to the content of Jesus' teaching in a few words. His major theme was the Kingdom of God, both foretold and enacted. He taught the values of this Kingdom and showed how they frequently differed greatly from the values of this world. In doing so, he affirmed the teaching of the Old Testament, but, rather than laying down long lists of additional rules to define legalistically the extent of this teaching (as many of his Jewish contemporaries did), he challenged people to examine the motives and attitudes behind their actions.

He taught people to value eternal realities over temporal concerns, to depend prayerfully on God, to be discerning, and to consider humbly the needs of others.

Perhaps Jesus' ethical teaching is best summed up in two brief statements. When asked which commandment was the greatest, he replied, "You shall love the Lord your God with all your heart, and with all your soul, and with all your mind and with all your strength. . . . You shall love your neighbor as yourself" (Mark 12:30-31 and parallels). He said that the entirety of the written Old Testament Law and the writings of the prophets hung on these two commandments. Elsewhere he also employed another kind of "umbrella statement" in entreating his audience: "In everything do to others as you would have them do to you" (Matthew 7:12 and Luke 6:31).

Jesus' teaching went beyond just ethics

Jesus also gave instructions regarding mission—the urgent task to preach the good news and to make disciples of all nations. Finally, he warned his hearers that there would come a time when he

The Beatitudes

Blessed are the poor in spirit, for theirs is the kingdom of heaven.
Blessed are those who mourn, for they will be comforted.
Blessed are the meek, for they will inherit the earth.
Blessed are those who hunger and thirst for righteousness, for they will be filled.
Blessed are the merciful, for they will receive mercy.
Blessed are the pure in heart, for they will see God.
Blessed are the peacemakers, for they will be called children of God.
Blessed are those who are persecuted for righteousness' sake, for theirs is the kingdom of heaven.
Blessed are you when people revile you and persecute you and utter all kinds of evil against you falsely on my account. Rejoice and be glad, for your reward is great in heaven, for in the same way they persecuted the prophets who were before you.
(Mt: 5.3–12)

would return to pass judgment. All were called (and still are) not only to believe in him and to accept his offered forgiveness, but also to demonstrate their love for him by acting it out in the real world. He suggested that, by serving the less fortunate members of society, one would be serving him (Matthew 25:31-46).

Jesus' style of teaching

Jesus did some teaching in the classic style, presenting argued propositions of truth, but most of his teaching was not like that. He knew the power of story, and used stories to present what he wanted to say in ways which were memorable and which frequently caught the listeners off-guard with surprising punch-lines.

These stories we know as parables, in which Jesus talked about one thing in order to explain something else. For example, he told two parables about the trouble to which people who had lost things went to recover them (sheep and coin), in order to show how much God cares about people who are lost (Luke 15). Similarly he told a parable about an enemy unexpectedly giving help to an injured man, in order to demonstrate how broadly we should define the concept of "neighbor" (Luke 10:29-37), and a parable about agriculture to illustrate different responses to his teaching (Mark 4:1-9 and parallels).

Jesus also taught using pithy, enigmatic, thought-provoking statements, frequently of the form, "the Kingdom of God is like . . .". We are told that he spoke with authority (Matthew 7:29 and Mark 1:22).

The setting of Jesus' teaching

Much of Jesus' teaching took place in rural settings, among common people, rather than among the teachers of the Law. Although he did deliver some longer teaching blocks, such as sermons (see, for example, the Sermon on the Mount in Matthew 5-7, or the Sermon on the Plain in Luke 6), much of his teaching came in informal settings as a response to people who approached him and asked him questions. It was also not uncommon for him to explain something he had said afterwards in private to his disciples (e.g., Mark 4:13-20 and parallels).

Today a basilica stands on the summit of the traditional "Mount of the Beatitudes", overlooking the Sea of Galilee.
***Inset*: Visitors pause on the slopes of the Mount of the Beatitudes to take in the view over the lake.**

Jesus the Healer

A blind beggar in modern Jerusalem.

Jesus did not just teach. In spite of the fact that many addressed him as "teacher", it was for his healing gift that most flocked to him. It does not seem to have been part of his main agenda—most of the time he wanted to teach—but he seemed to have an authority to heal, and was compassionate enough to want to respond to human need when it presented itself.

What did he heal?

Jesus healed people of a wide variety of sicknesses. In the four Gospels we have over twenty stories of healings, some of individuals and some of groups. There are also a number of summaries that allude to much healing activity, without providing details—phrases such as, "He cured many who were sick with various diseases" (Mark 1:34) or "and cured all who were sick" (Matthew 8:16). Afflictions specifically mentioned include paralysis, leprosy, chronic hemorrhaging, deafness, impaired speech, blindness, epilepsy, chronically bent back, oedema, and fever.

In addition we also have one recorded incident of Jesus' restoring a severed ear (Luke 22:51), and three incidents of his raising the dead—Jairus' daughter (Mark 5:41), the widow's son (Luke 7:14), and Lazarus (John 11:43). With the last example, the Gospel writer underlines the indisputability of the dead man's state by informing us that the death had occurred four days prior to Jesus' arrival.

Who did he heal?

In spite of the summary statements that allude to large numbers of unreported healings, it is nevertheless the case that not everyone in the region was healed by Jesus. Much of Jesus' healing activity seems to be focused on restoring to community those whose sicknesses had excluded them. So, for example, no one would go near a person with a skin disease, for fear of contamination, but Jesus deliberately touched a leprosy sufferer in order to bring healing (Mark 1:40-44 and parallels). Part of the healing process was to visit the priest to be declared clean and therefore in a position to be reintegrated into society.

Similarly, the hemorrhaging woman (Mark 5:25-34 and parallels) would have been considered ritually unclean; and there was a view, as expressed in

An artist's impression of Jesus healing in the narrow streets of ancient Jerusalem.

A crippled woman is brought to Jesus for healing through the crowds of a city street; after the painting by J. J. Tissot.

the debate between Jesus and the Pharisees in John 9, that a man born blind was being punished for sin, and would therefore be ostracized. Jesus restored him not only to sight, but also to society. Jesus also healed other outsiders, such as the son of the Gentile Roman centurion (Matthew 8:5-13 and Luke 7:1-10), while the one who was affirmed, in the healing of the ten leprosy sufferers, was a Samaritan (Luke 17:15).

How did he heal?

Jesus used no single technique to bring about healing, but the process was usually simple and undramatic (on only one occasion was it more than a one-stage process). Frequently he touched the afflicted person (e.g., Peter's mother-in-law in Matthew 8:15), and some were healed simply by touching the fringe of his cloak (Matthew 14:36 and Mark 6:56). On one occasion healing occurred in this way without Jesus intending it, when the hemorrhaging woman pressed through the crowd and managed to touch him.

But touch was not the only means he used to heal. On a couple of occasions Jesus used saliva—and even mud—as a kind of ointment. More important than the mechanics of the healings were the words he used. On at least one occasion, Jesus pronounced the forgiveness of sins as part of the healing process (Mark 2:5 and parallels). It seems that the person's paralysis was in some way connected to the spiritual burden he was carrying.

When did he heal?

Jesus never forced healing upon anyone, but only carried out healing when he was approached to do so. He specifically asked the blind beggar, Bartimaeus, what he wanted him to do. He congratulated supplicants on their faith, such as the hemorrhaging woman, to whom Jesus said, "Daughter, your faith has made you well; go in peace, and be healed of your disease."

When there was an absence of faith, Jesus did few works of power, as in Nazareth (Matthew 13:58 and Mark 6:5). On at least three occasions, Jesus performed healings on the Sabbath, even though some thought that he shouldn't because it constituted banned work. For Jesus it was more important to do good than to observe that regulation.

Sometimes spiritual lessons accompanied the healings. For example, Jesus claimed that a particular man was born blind "so that God's works might be revealed in him" (John 9:3). After completing the healing, Jesus contrasted the man's ability to see with the spiritual blindness of the Pharisees.

Jesus' Power

Jesus demonstrated miraculous power in other ways as well as healings. Perhaps the most significant was in the area of exorcism.

Confronting spirits

One kind of healing by Jesus stood apart from the others: where the cause of the suffering was not a physical ailment, but spiritual oppression. Sometimes we are simply told that the person has an unclean spirit or a demon, while elsewhere we are told that the oppression has specific physical manifestations, such as dumbness, blindness, epilepsy, or mental disorder. On each occasion Jesus confronted the evil spirit, rebuked it, and ordered it to leave.

After an exit that was sometimes straightforward, and sometimes very violent, the sufferer was freed. With the boy in Mark 9 and parallels the exorcism was so brutal that the boy appeared to be left dead, until Jesus took him by the hand and gently lifted him onto his feet. With the Gerasene demoniac of Mark 5 and parallels, the man who had been oppressed by many evil spirits and who had roamed around naked and uncontrollable, was left "sitting there, clothed and in his right mind".

The seemingly ironic point about the encounters with the evil spirits is that, whereas Jesus was frequently unable to make humans obey his commands (e.g., Mark 1:43-45), the evil spirits were always submissively compliant. This is best explained by the reaction of the spirit in the synagogue at Capernaum when it saw Jesus: "What have you to do with us, Jesus of Nazareth? Have you come to destroy us? I know who you are, the Holy One of God" (Mark 1:24 and Luke 4:34). Those from the spiritual realm knew who Jesus was, and knowing this, were in awe of him. For human beings, by contrast, Jesus' identity was only revealed at the end of his earthly life.

This authority over evil spirits was not something that Jesus kept to himself. He passed this authority on to his disciples when they went out on mission. Sometimes they succeeded (Mark 6:13), but sometimes they were unable to follow their master's example (Mark 9:17-18). The ease with which Jesus controlled demons led some to suspect that he was working in league with Satan (Matthew 12:24), but Jesus powerfully refuted this argument.

This mosaic of the loaves and fishes is near the Sea of Galilee.

A powerful modern representation of Jesus healing, beside the Sea of Galilee.

Nature miracles

Jesus also demonstrated his power over nature in extraordinary ways. Over the four Gospels, we have six different accounts of Jesus' feeding a vast multitude of people with very little food. The circumstances were the same each time. A large crowd had gathered in a remote, rural location to hear Jesus teach, and he recognized that, although there was nowhere nearby to buy food, they needed to be fed. Jesus took the little that was available and multiplied it so that it would be enough. Thus on one occasion he fed five thousand men with five small loaves of bread and two fish, and on another occasion, he fed four thousand men with seven loaves and a few fish. (These numbers only include the men. We don't know how many hungry mouths of women and children were there!)

Jesus also revealed something of who he was to his disciples by causing miraculous catches of fish for them (Luke 5:1-11 and John 21:1-11), and by walking on the water of the lake (Matthew 14:22-33 and parallels). To these same people he demonstrated his power over the elements by causing a great storm to abate when they were out in a boat that looked as if it might capsize (Mark 4:35-41 and parallels). Apparently more trivially, he even changed six enormous stone jars of water into the finest wine, when the wine ran out at a friend's wedding. As the Gospel writer John explained, this was not primarily to keep the party going and to make the bridegroom look good in the eyes of his guests (although that was doubtless the effect!), but to reveal Jesus' glory and to cause his disciples to believe in him (John 2:11).

Of course the most important miracle that Jesus performed was to rise from the dead. As we saw earlier, in doing so, he paid the price for sin, defeated death, and opened the way for the eventual resurrection of others.

"Who then is this, that even the wind and the sea obey him?"
(Mark 4:41)

Jesus' Disciples

The call to discipleship

Follow me, and I will make you fish for people.
(Mark 1:17)

Jesus was rarely alone. Wherever he went, he attracted a crowd around him. Some were actively opposed to him, as we shall see in the next section. Some were there simply because they wanted to get something out of him, such as a healing. Others wanted to hear what he said and were supportive of his ministry. The group of those who surrounded him and followed him was of an indeterminate number, but Jesus chose twelve followers to be his special disciples.

The privilege of discipleship

It was unusual for a teacher to choose his disciples. Normally pupils would choose which teacher they wished to attach themselves to, but Jesus called his disciples from a variety of occupations, and immediately they followed him (e.g., Matthew 4:18-22 and Mark 1:16-20).

Having selected his disciples, Jesus invested a great deal of time and emotional energy in them. He allowed them to witness extraordinary miracles and healings, he withdrew with them for rest and refreshment (e.g. Mark 6:32 and parallels), and he gave them more teaching than anyone else.

This he did in two ways. First, he gave some sections of teaching just to them, and secondly, he sometimes explained to them in more detail in private what he had said to the crowds in public. For example, the explanation of the Parable of the Sower was given only to the disciples (on this occasion more than just the twelve), when they asked him to explain (Mark 4:13-20). Perhaps they had heard him tell the story on several occasions and they still couldn't grasp what he was talking about.

There was also an inner circle of disciples. Simon Peter, James, and John were taken even more closely into Jesus' confidence. It was this inner group that were present at Jesus' transfiguration (Mark 9:2-9 and parallels), and it was to this inner group that Jesus turned at his time of greatest need in Gethsemane (Matthew 26:36-46 and Mark 14:32-42). Within this group, Simon Peter stood apart. In the Gospel accounts we have, he is by far the most developed character of the twelve and speaks many more lines, frequently as a spokesman for the other disciples.

A fisherman casts his net on Galilee.

The cloud-capped summit of Mount Hermon, possible site of Jesus' transfiguration.

The cost of discipleship

But there was a cost to discipleship also. The disciples abandoned their families, livelihoods, and all security to follow Jesus. He assured them that their reward for giving up such things would be great (Mark 10:29-30 and parallels), but in doing so, he underlined the extent of what they were leaving behind, and even suggested that one of the rewards was persecution.

Jesus required his disciples to consider carefully the cost of

J. J. Tissot portrays Jesus teaching the twelve in the Galilean countryside.

following him (Luke 14:27-28), that allegiance to him needed to come above everything and everyone else (Matthew 10:37-38 and Luke 14:25-26). He stressed that the priorities of the Kingdom were not the same as the priorities of the world. He declared that if one chose to "lose" one's life for his sake, one would in fact end up saving it (Mark 8:35 and parallels).

Success and failure

Jesus' disciples were trusting of their master, and appeared to enjoy early success in their ministry.

The cost of discipleship

If any want to become my followers, let them deny themselves and take up their cross and follow me.
(Mark 8:34)

When he sent them out on a mission on their own, they returned having preached the good news, cast out demons, and cured the sick, just as Jesus did (Mark 6:13 and Luke 9:6). Furthermore, Simon Peter was the first to recognize that Jesus was the Messiah (Mark 8:29 and parallels).

However, the overall portrait painted of the disciples is not a glowing one. First, they never seemed fully to grasp what Jesus was trying to tell them. This is shown most clearly by two of the occasions when Jesus predicted what was going to happen to him in Jerusalem. He underlined the way in which his path was to be the path of suffering and humility. Yet the disciples were more interested in which of them was the greatest (Mark 9:34 and parallels), and who would get special privileges in the wake of Jesus' glory (Mark 10:37).

Secondly, when the going got tough, the disciples melted away. In spite of their protestations that they would remain faithful to him to the end, Judas betrayed him, Simon Peter denied him, and the rest deserted him and fled.

With hindsight, we know that Simon Peter repented and was forgiven and reinstated (John 21). We also know that the other disciples continued to serve Jesus after his death. Many scholars believe that, in presenting a portrait of the disciples "warts and all", the Gospel writers (particularly Mark) have encouraged all future followers of Jesus: the disciples were not elite supermen, but just ordinary people touched by encounter with Jesus.

Jesus' Opponents

To the masses, Jesus was something of a hero. He took an interest in them, he offered them hope, and he healed many of their diseases. But he was not so popular with those in positions of authority. They became increasingly hostile towards him, engaged him in rigorous debate, and sought to find ways to destroy him.

Who were Jesus' opponents?

The Gospel writers mention several different groups of opponents in various combinations. They can be divided into two main camps. The first camp contained the scribes and Pharisees. They were interpreters and teachers of Jewish Law. They were devoutly religious and took the Law very seriously, to the extent that they defended and debated a whole raft of extra laws and interpretations (halakah), which were there as a kind of protective fence around the Torah of the scriptures, to ensure that it was not broken. Their area of influence was not dependent on the Temple, and so they operated throughout the region.

In Jerusalem we find the second camp—the Sadducees and priests. We know little about the Sadducees, apart from the fact that they rejected halakah, and did not believe in the resurrection of the dead. It is widely believed that many of them were associated with the priesthood and were establishment figures in the Roman-occupied city. Therefore, they probably had more to lose from anyone rocking the boat. The priests ran the enormous enterprise that was the Temple.

Other groups are mentioned as in opposition to Jesus about whom we know very little (Herodians and elders), while yet other groups of the period (Essenes and Zealots) do not seem to have come into contact with Jesus. Two individuals were not supportive of Jesus, but cannot be classified as opponents. The disciple, Judas, went behind Jesus' back to betray him, and the Roman governor, Pilate, sentenced him to death, but this was for reasons of political expediency rather than because he actively opposed him (Matthew 27:22-24 and parallels).

In the spiritual realm, Jesus was opposed by Satan, who tempted him in the wilderness to abandon his ministry before it had even begun (Matthew 4:1-11 and Luke 4:1-13). According to Luke's account, the devil then left him "until an opportune time" (Luke 4:13). That time came in Jerusalem when he "entered into Judas" and Judas betrayed Jesus to the authorities (Luke 22:3).

Why were people opposed to Jesus?

The scribes and Pharisees considered Jesus to be a law-breaker. To highlight just three examples, he healed people on the Sabbath on several occasions (e.g., Luke 6:6-11; 13:10-17; 14:1-6), he did not observe laws about ceremonial washing (Matthew 15:1-20 and Mark 7:1-8), and he forgave sins—which was blasphemy, for only God could forgive sins (Mark 2:5-7 and parallels). Jesus responded by stating that doing good was more important than Sabbath observance, and that it was not through eating that one could defile oneself. As for forgiveness, it was precisely because he was God that he could offer it.

Jesus was a threat to all in positions of power because he was popular with the masses. The crowds found his teaching to be more authoritative than that of the teachers of the Law (Mark 1:22 and parallels) and they flocked to him. In Jerusalem, he appeared to attack the very institution of the Temple, on which the whole of economic and religious life was built (Mark 11:15-19 and parallels).

Jesus and the scribes

They were astounded at his teaching, for he taught them as one having authority, and not as the scribes. (Mark 1:22)

Christ before Caiaphas by Gerrit van Honthorst.

What did Jesus' opponents do?

Opposition manifested itself most commonly in the form of public challenge, in which the opponents asked questions designed to catch Jesus out, and make him look small in the eyes of the crowd. This motivation is frequently implicit, but is made explicit in Mark 12:13 and parallels—they came to "trap him in what he said". Thus they asked him apparently "no-win" questions about such topics as the authority with which he spoke or his attitude towards government taxation. Each time Jesus was able to turn the argument on its head and come out on top.

But there was a more sinister side to the opposition. From an early stage, opponents were intent on destroying him (Mark 3:6 and parallels), and in Jerusalem, their reluctance to arrest and kill him was simply a result of the presence of so many people for the Passover festival (Mark 14:2 and parallels). When they arrested him, they did it at night, thanks to a tip-off from Judas, and when it looked as if Pilate might release him, it was the priests who stirred up the crowd to prevent clemency (Matthew 27:15-26 and Mark 15:6-15).

Jesus' Legacy

Christian believers on Good Friday on the *Via Dolorosa*, Jerusalem.

The Spirit empowers the disciples

You will receive power when the Holy Spirit has come upon you; and you will be my witnesses in Jerusalem, in all Judea and Samaria, and to the ends of the earth.
(Acts 1:8)

We saw earlier that Jesus' death did not mark the end of his life, as he rose from the dead and made a series of appearances over a forty-day period, before ascending into heaven, to be seated at God's right hand (Luke 22:69). But neither was that the end.

Living on through his disciples

Jesus invested a great deal in his disciples and commanded them to continue his teaching. As they did so, they focused much of their teaching on the implications of Jesus' death and resurrection, calling their hearers to repent, be baptized, and become his followers.

The sequel to Luke's Gospel, the book of Acts, underlines the success of the new movement (e.g., Acts 2:47; 6:7; 9:31). Not only did the disciples continue to preach and teach, but, as Jesus had predicted (John 14:12), they also carried out miraculous acts of healing. For example, in the name of Jesus, Peter and John healed a beggar who had been lame from birth (Acts 3:6), and some people were healed of diseases and demon oppression simply by touching a cloth that the apostle Paul had touched (Acts 19:12).

When they were with Jesus, these people were known as disciples, reflecting their status as learners. They then became known as apostles ("sent ones"), as they were sent out into the world by Jesus. These simple folk, who frequently got it wrong when following Jesus, became seemingly fearless heroes. They underwent great affliction for the cause and many of them were killed, but they remained resolute.

Living on through the Holy Spirit

It was through the Holy Spirit that the disciples were transformed. Jesus informed them that the Father would send another one like him to be with them, to continue to teach them and empower them—the Holy Spirit (see John 14-16). Jesus called him a parakletos, a helper/comforter or advocate—one called alongside to assist them.

As Jesus left, he instructed the disciples to remain in Jerusalem to receive this equipping (Acts 1:4), and shortly afterwards they were each filled with the Holy Spirit (Acts 2:4). It is important to recognize that this Spirit was not some vague nebulous force, but the Spirit of Jesus (Acts 16:7). He continued to be intimately involved in all that they did.

Living on through the church

As more and more people came to be followers of Jesus, the movement outgrew its Jewish roots and welcomed non-Jews (Gentiles) into the fold. This, combined with the sheer scale and geographical spread of those who now called themselves "Christians", led to various complications and disputes. Apostles such as Paul and Peter wrote letters to gatherings of Christians (called "churches"), to instruct them and settle these matters, and the Gospel writers decided to write down accounts of Jesus' life.

These letters and accounts were eventually gathered together into the collection of twenty-seven documents that we call the New Testament. This book has been the primary source of inspiration for Christians ever since. In all these developments, Jesus' promise remains the same: "Where two or three are gathered in my name, I am there among them" (Matthew 18:20).

Living on until the End

Jesus' view of end-times was based on Jewish expectations. There would be resurrection of the dead and judgment, with reward for the righteous and recompense for the

Where did everyone come from on the day of Pentecost?

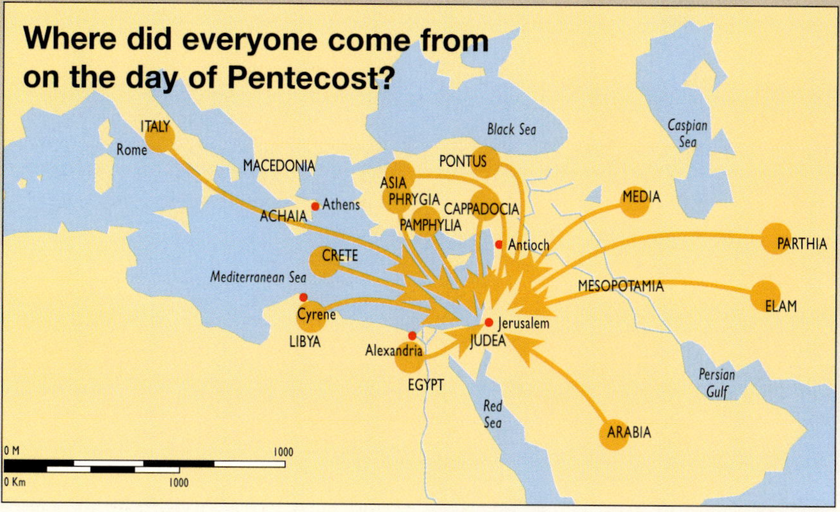

Jesus' promise to the disciples

Where two or three are gathered in my name, I am there among them.
(Mt. 18:20)

Jesus commissions the disciples

Go therefore and make disciples of all nations, baptizing them in the name of the Father and of the Son and of the Holy Spirit, and teaching them to obey everything that I have commanded you. And remember, I am with you always, to the end of the age.
(Mt. 28:19-20)

wicked. The one difference involved his role. In apocalyptic language, he described to his disciples the afflictions, natural disasters, human crises, and strange signs that would mark the last days, and then predicted that he would come at that time with great power and glory, to gather his chosen ones together.

Jesus did not say when this would be, and even told them that he did not know the day and hour himself (Mark 13:32 and parallels). Instead, in a series of parables and sayings, he exhorted them to stay alert in a state of readiness and to be good stewards of all that had been entrusted to them. To this day, Christians all around the world are called to do the same.

Christianity c A.D. 300

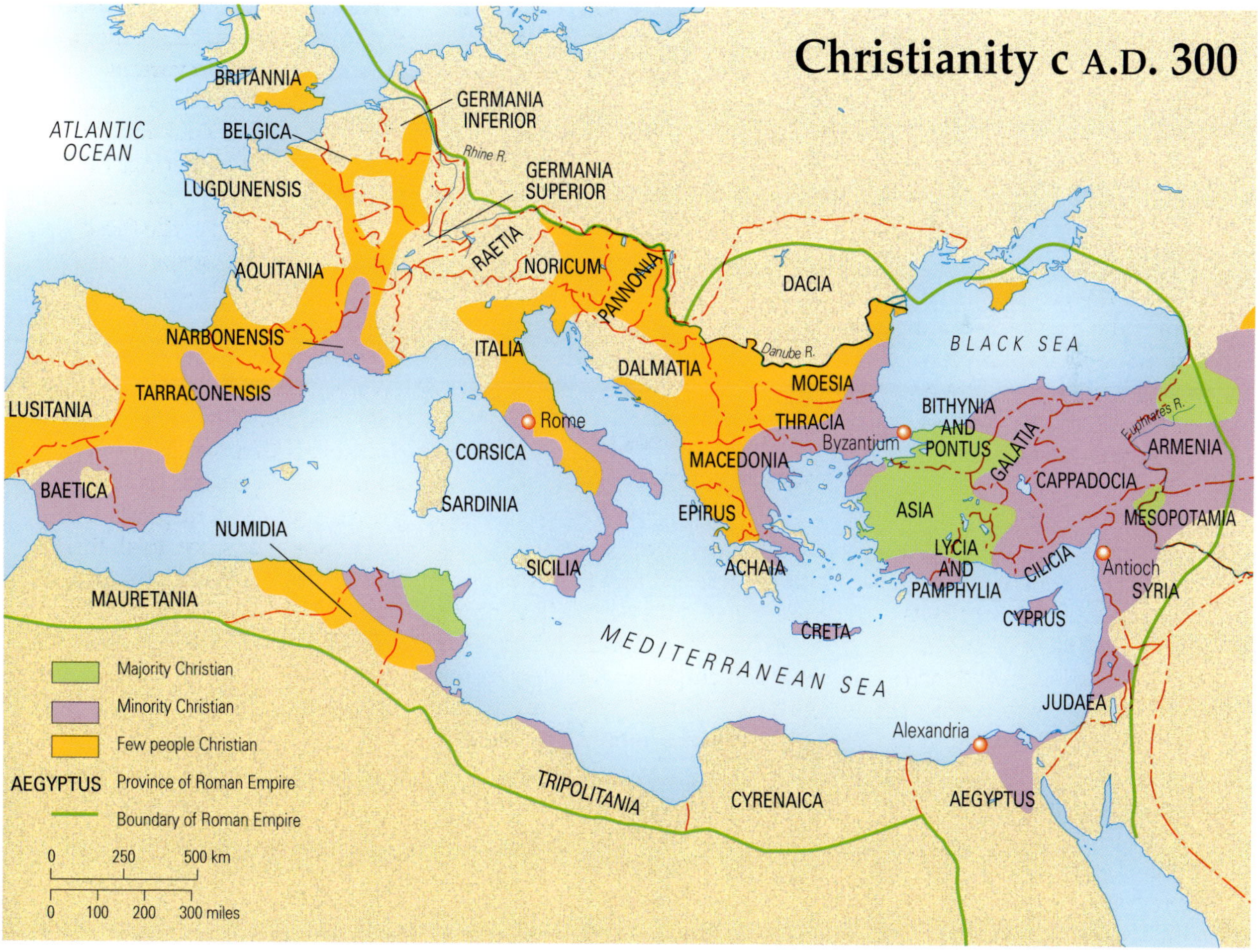

Index